# Anna and Her Daughters

*poems by*

# Marie Gray Wise

*Finishing Line Press*
Georgetown, Kentucky

*For Anna and her daughters*
*Maria, Adeline, Carmelina, Blanche, and Anna*

*and of course*

*For my three wisemen*
*Dan, Josh, and Matt*
*Always*

ACKNOWLEDGMENTS

Thank you to these six journals that originally published some of this work:

*I-70 Review*—"Birthright"
*Naugatuck River Review*: "My Grandmother Glitters" originally published as
"My Grandmother Glitters in Her Coffin"
*U.S. 1 Worksheets*: "Searching for Anna" originally published as "Italian
Melodies" and "The House on Brown Street"
*Paterson Literary Review*: "Gatherings" and "Not Just Shiny Things"
*Schuylkill River Review*: "A Last Picture"
*The Café Review*: "In Another Room"

Special thanks to Lois Marie Harrod, without whom, these poems would
not have been written or collected (at least not in this decade). Besides her
expansive knowledge and experience, Lois creates an environment where
poets with shy souls can reveal themselves and grow—an invaluable gift.


Publisher: Leah Huete de Maines
Editor: Christen Kincaid
Cover Art and Interior Photos: Marie Gray Wise
Author Photo: Marie Gray Wise
Cover Design: Elizabeth Maines McCleavy


Order online: www.finishinglinepress.com
also available on amazon.com

Author inquiries and mail orders:
Finishing Line Press
PO Box 1626
Georgetown, Kentucky 40324
USA

# Contents

**Searching for Anna**

Back in a family apartment in New Haven
my great-grandmother Anna's picture
hangs in an oval frame high in a bedroom corner,
her dark hair pulled back in a bun from her dignified face.

In an Italian piazza in front of an ancient church
I listen hard to recognize fragments of Italian,
trying to make Anna's solemn portrait speak to me.

But my scant Italian shrinks
from the crowds of vowels
that dance swiftly from their mouths
in words that seem to have no beginning or ending—
*formaggiocolosseooggi.*

Then something familiar floats on the summer air.
In the voices soaring on roller coasters of inflection,
I recognize the lilt of my grandmother and her sisters.

And I realize that though I don't understand Anna's words
I've always known her rhythm.

# Anna's Daughter, Maria—
# my Grandmother

## Not Just Shiny Things

My grandmother had jewels long before she married the gambler.
Earned them by trudging through the pre-dawn—
a small woman wheeling her tractor-like Oldsmobile
over the barely visible Delaware
down through Chinatown
to a red brick factory at 12th and Race
where she sewed hems all day.

Once, when the car broke down
she struck out through snow
to the bus. She had to get there
to treadle her way to *diamanti* and *granati*
for her own sake, and for her daughters and granddaughters—
shining signs that this immigrants' daughter has made it—
there is no poverty here.

Meeting her jilted gambler thirty years later
she took a promise from his mouth
for an engagement diamond
as large as Mia Farrow's nine-carat rock—
and got it. She knew her worth.

**Old Photo of New Year's Eve**

On the top step Nanny stands
in a flowered housedress.
Her nightly bandanna
covers her weekly bouffant
while her arms flap like a mummer.
Beside her, Eddie holds
a whiskey bottle like a guitar.

One step down,
Mom models a sleek black dress
with a sparkly silver belt
and holds a slim glass in her hand.
Dad too is dressed up—
white shirt and dress slacks.
And he parades with me and my sister
at the bottom of the steps
while we slap spoons
against pots and pans and lids.

I still feel how we kids
were happy to be up so late
yet shy of the adults
flouncing so free and merry
in the cold air
in the porch light
in front of my grandmother's house.

## Tornado

My grandmother's songs and curses
spiraled like two storms
one inside the other
churned by her furious movements.

As her sewing machine thumped away
she hummed inside the riot of the dress factory
shooting hems through the bullseye foot
in short bursts like a machine gun.

At the Caldwell Dress Christmas party
she left her smock curled at the machine
replaced the required hairnet
with a paper hat
to dance and lead the singing.

In her giant Oldsmobile
she pummeled the gas pedal
and sang along with Dino
until someone cut her off—
and instant curses fell in English
and Italian and made the car blush.

She swept into our house—
or indeed, any room anywhere—
stirred dusty lethargy into guilt
stoked laziness into movement
and set off every atom in reach.

Her energy and desires
carved out our cravings—
her actions filled them.

**Above the Boxy Television Set**

In my Grandmother's house
a "painting" hangs, bigger than its screen
full of twirling pastel dresses.

A ballroom, European perhaps
where officers with golden epaulets
lead their ladies around the floor.

The couple in front rock toward us
their arms raised shoulder-height
their eyes and clasped hands pointed toward the floor.

The old-world sentiment clashes
with the modern kidney-shaped couches
and the stiff shaded lamps with Picasso-like scratches.

This sentimental scene was not found
in her childhood home without books
but seen perhaps taped to a schoolroom wall

before she was pulled from eighth grade
to stack fruit in her father's store
and care for the new baby after her mother died.

It is on such glimpses our desires grow.

**Threads**

My picture of that day in the Fort Dix Testing Office is clear:
the phone call at the Sergeant's desk
the news about my grandfather's death—
me crying in the cozy bathroom
with its orangey cedar wood
and gaudy gold curtains
the Major's wife had made.

But there is another picture in Philadelphia I didn't see:
My parents walking toward my grandmother
down the aisle of the dress factory
over wisps of thread
through strewn bits of gaudy gold and night-like blues
that made the floor vibrant as a starlit sky.

When my grandmother sees them
her sturdy hands release the dress
she's racing under the presser foot
and collapse into rare stillness in her lap
and quickly as one stitch follows another
my parents disappear
and she sees no one crossing the room
and feels nothing but a floating sensation
as if adrift on some chapel ceiling.

They place the coat on her shoulders
and lead her past one machine after another
each pausing its thunderous treadle as she passes,
but her eyes focus on the floor
where gaudy golds and night-like blues
blur and fade into unalterable grey.

## The Baby's Room

As I spread the sheet
on the single bed
in the baby's room
for my grandmother
I wonder if
the circle occurs to her.

How, near the end
she's come back
from the full bed
to a room where lambs
prance across the walls
through blue and pink clouds.

But the morning brings
no realization
only the same silent stares
through conversations
bending around her.

## A Last Picture

She used to start trouble
at every family gathering:
her compulsive energy
had to go somewhere.

This past Mother's Day
she was reduced to discussing
the wonderful taste of grapes,
the many uses of a tin can,
and the flight of foam butterflies
across the refrigerator door.

She didn't care about
the length of her skirt
or that the blouse didn't match.
She struggled to keep her eyes open
and to find that sociability
she used to thrust on anyone.

This is a hard picture
to close the book with—
I want once more
to see her impulsiveness
bursting through every expletive.

## Gatherings

Hands would work when the mind remembered clean,
gathering nylon panties in each fist,
rubbing briskly before the wringing twist
and star-water* soak would close the routine.
She'd display for her grandchildren stacks of green
and white washcloths and offer a detailed list
of soaps and perfumes, then dismiss
us with laughs, foreign curses in between.
Now she cackles and curses quietly,
palming candy, small change, and cigarettes,
and she screams when placed into the bath by
daughters and caretakers, stares fearfully
at dry cloths writhing as they become wet,
hands inert and mind not gathering why.

*star-water—bleach

## Piece Work

Beside the East River
in a high-ceilinged hospital room
my grandmother unconsciously scanned
from window to door, her eyes
finally resting on me at the foot of the bed.
Her face looked strange without her glasses—
Were her eyes always steel grey?
Could she see me?
Did she ever see me?

For years she and her third husband
came to dinner every Wednesday.
A magician of motion
she bustled even when she sat—
adjusted knickknacks and mail
pulled small gifts from brown bags—
blue thread of every hue
silky fabric with tiny old-lady flowers
and Tastykake cherry pies.
Her many gifts churned our desires
feathered our childhood.

Later I learned who she really was—
complicated, flawed, tough.
The fastest piece worker in her factory
she flew delicate dress hems through her machine
with the precision of a bombardier.

When I went to college and read great books
and thought great thoughts
I judged her unable to recognize the new, real me
and deemed her old love uneducated and cheap.

As we buried her, pieces of questions
I'd pushed away, swarmed in—
Had I become to her, the stranger she'd seemed to me?

Why was it important she know me as I demanded?
Is it only a child's gift to receive love freely?
Why did I run from hers?

As I reach into mornings like she never will again
I search for priest, philosopher, or poet—
anyone—who can help me piece the answers together.

## My Grandmother Glitters

My grandmother glitters in her coffin
in a turquoise sequined dress.
Her daughters prepared her
less for the sandy South Jersey she will rest in,
more for Judgment Day in Las Vegas
where she can step out ready to follow
Husband-Number-Four from blackjack to poker
without pausing to change her clothes.

She would have liked that.

Her sisters—wrinkled and feisty,
walk heavily to the coffin. They don't kneel,
but chat in deep, tenorish Italian phrases,
adjusting the dress by pulling on its hem
until the sequins shake and sparkle
riotously beside their dull cloth.

One Great-Aunt grasps the casket's edge
with a hand like a knotted branch,
the other lifts the blanket covering my grandmother's feet.
Their shoulders rise and I can hear their gasps.

Back in their seats behind me they mumble
about how she should be wearing shoes,
about how it's bad luck.
Their husky voices bend and fly
in Italian and English about
our lax Italian traditions.

I wonder if their disapproval isn't also satisfaction
that their eldest sister's funeral is not perfect.

To drown them out,
I picture my grandmother
stalking the small rectangle of earth
she will share with Husband-Number-Three,
her face a familiar scowl of impatience,
her voice full of complaint
because she has to stand around,
worried about what she should do.

I worry too that the afterlife will be confusing for her.
Will she hop back and forth among husbands,
one week here, the next week there?

Will she change from sequins
into an old housedress
for the small house with the back porch
where she'll swirl into cooking and cleaning,
where Husband-Three will sooth her,
"Now, Mary…" so she'll settle down for a moment?

At the cemetery I watch the disapproving sisters
stand in the bright sun and understand
that two of the four husbands were successes—
each one revealing her intolerance of pain
each one a decision in her journey for a better life.

# Anna's Granddaughter, Julia— my Mother

## The House on Brown Street

I want to sit in that apartment
in a year I didn't exist—
in the corner of that worn kitchen
behind the massive iron stove
within the aroma of simmering tomato sauce.

I want the language to wash over me—
the voices of my grandmother and her family—
their billows of un-sleek, second-hand Italian
their vowels puffing around the room
the tilt of their sentences aimed at the ceiling.

I want to sit like my mother and her sister
within the rush of those buffeting words
inside the surge of emotions unchecked—
gruff, brazen, proud—
inside their refusal to be drowned.

## Long Wharf

My mother was a little girl with wild curls and whooping cough
when her grandfather Pasquale took her hand each morning
and led her to walk by the sea
framed by pink granite jetties at Long Wharf.

And each time we pass this Connecticut Turnpike exit
on our way to her family, she talks about that walk.

"He'd say, 'Breathe, bambina, breathe.'"

She adds, "Which was more than my father ever did"—
him who made her and Vicky, eight and nine
walk from Wooster Square across New Haven
to a luncheonette on Broadway for Yalies.

"All that way and all he'd give us was a lousy quarter
and he never even offered us a measly glass of water.
But Uncle Albert gave us hot chocolate."

She looks toward the neighborhood again
where her old house and the wharf
are separated now by the twists of the interstate
and repeats, "Breathe, bambina, breathe"
as if it were a priceless legacy.

## Heritage

At the edge of New Jersey's Pine Barrens
in a four-roomed ranch house
at the back of the fridge
the grated provolone
sat fluffy and sacred
in a green ridged jar.

Precious flakes
fell in fragrant snowfall
on steamy red sauce,
each sharp whiff
reminding us
where we came from.

In the green ridged jar
at the back of the fridge
my mother kept Italy close.

## In Another Room

In the living room, my mother groans,
staring at a small Blessed Mother statue,
turning her head from side to side—
an equilibrium exercise—
all counterpointed with a description of pain
and a lament twice as long.

In the kitchen, I scrub the counter harder
tell myself to take her seriously
because she is old. But I treat her complaint
like an old recording—no—
like an echo—
of the sobs that oozed
from beneath the bedroom door
when my baby brother died.

My ears are full of tears
shed thirty years ago.
Why won't she be quiet
behind that door?
Why won't she wipe her eyes
and ask about me?

## My Mother Invites Me to Complain

Almost every conversation
begins the same—
how pale or tired I look
am I getting enough sleep.

I barely finish my refutations
when she responds
how she's not getting enough
because the shingles
strangles her entire life.

The pause is next
the wait for my chiming in
for bemoaning and whining
worthy of her daughter—
for my signing on
to widows' woes
we have a right to.

I ask how her neighbor is doing.

**Two Days Later**

I should write a poem about my mother dying two days ago. But do I really need to chronicle our struggles—her pulling me backward and grasping hard with hands so much broader than mine—Italian peasant hands. Her mother's maiden name translates to "fig," and I imagine lines of ancestors watering and pruning and picking in that small utilitarian town Pogerola above the dressy Amalfi Coast. They'd have worked in terraced groves in that steep terrain. Practicing the gritty routine of farming and resting with glances at the beautiful sea below. My own smaller hands always reached outward in that chronic universal situation. I want to remove the angry smoke screen to actually see her, but it will take time for it to dissolve. I should feel numb or sad. But what remains is guilt.

## Birthright

I am more Italian now
my mother has gone.

I catch glimpses of her favorite show
*Lidia's Kitchen.*
I set out pretty antipasto for Christmas—
strips of marinated red peppers
beside slices of sharp provolone
disks of crusty bread between
olives and tuna glistening on lettuce.

I craft frail snow-flake-like pizzelles
and bake and re-bake heartiness into biscotti
while Lou Monte plays in the background
translating "Crazy Mary"
for us third generation paisans
who speak only "British".

If mom could see me now
she would be a Vesuvius of pleasure.
With her blue eyes and their sharp sparkle
she'd prance around
as if she had planned to be born Italian
as if she invented pasta and pizza
as if she had stood beside Bernini
and told him how to chisel the river gods
in the Piazza Navona—
                              all just for me.

# The Rest of Us
## Other Daughters—
## Granddaughters—Great-Granddaughters

## The Great-Aunts

the blue and orange lawn chairs
where my great-aunts sit
compliment and contrast each other—
like them—one rough, one sweet
one with the sometimes scowl
the other whose face always looks for a joke.

together, their lush voices rise
and ring with eternal excitement
that amplifies this sweet July
beneath hot trees—
and refresh like quick summer rains.

## One Easter

My sister stands on a concrete island
in the middle of the rest-stop blacktop.
Her brown hair touches her shoulders
and she wears shorts and a sleeveless top.
A clanky gold necklace dangles and
she carries a purse in one hand
and holds my wiry two-year-old brother
with the other as they look into the camera.

We have stopped for a picnic
on the way to my aunt's house—
which entire entity will be arranged "just so"
and neater than any one corner of ours.

My aunt's furniture doesn't come from Grants,
and she never shops in bargain basements,
and there's a microscope in each room
to examine the behavior of our sub-species.
We are always judged inadequate
and are happier when we leave
than when we arrive.

**My Sister's Head**

My sister agrees to my exploration of her head, and we set off to the garage where she takes a large piece of orange metal from the corner and unfolds it into Dad's old Volkswagen Beetle. We hop in, the car shrinks, and we buzz through her ear into a brightly lit space with a pink stucco apartment building. Windchimes greet us as the car rumbles up the steps to the directory: Floor 1—Old Things; Floor 2—Jewels; Floor 3—Feelings and Thoughts.

The must of dust meets us in the first apartment as we look at a photo of the very car we're riding in. Circa 1970, the creaking body should be dragged to the junk heap, but she keeps it because it was Dad's. Next, a replica of the black and white TV set in her sunroom. About the size of an old computer monitor, it's perfect for her Turner Movie Classics with Bette Davis. "It still works," she says with a shrug. I discover things I haven't seen for years with descriptive cards: Two-ring Inflatable Pool, Philadelphia Rowhouse, 1954; Bedroom Added on by Dad, Complete With Corner Desks from Sears; The Wizard of Oz, Borrowed From Library at Ten (and never returned).

In the second-floor apartment, we vroom through heaps of jewelry boxes—stacked against the walls and in the middle like library shelves—which makes sense because she used to work in one. In one drawer, my mother's round silver earrings with aquamarine stones. In another, a pearl on a delicate chain. "You wore that when you went to the prom with Jimmy Hernandez," she says. Then new things from Amazon or Etsy. Big, chunky, dramatic necklaces that she carries off well. And way in the back, the crown jewel—not a figment of speech, but literally, a platinum crown with a garnet labeled Queen of the Non-Sequitur.

A scent of roses mixes with the sunlight on the top floor. Room after room of thoughts and feelings—each in its separate abode and not allowed to communicate with the others. When I ask why not, she throws her hands up. Some doors are labeled: Sadness, Joy, Disappointment, Humility. Three Thumbelina-sized rooms sit on top of each other: Confidence, Follow Through, and Logic.

Her kind. The kind that texts "I've got a heart problem" followed by "William Shatner's going into space!" Or a complaint about ShopRite's home delivery and "Tiny Tim has a magnificent voice!" Hence, her crown and title. The last rooms are where she spends most of her time—Laughter No Matter What Disaster Befalls, and Hopefulness Despite All Facts.

We zip back to the garage and refold the car into the corner. I shake my head and say, "I still don't understand you." She juts her chin a bit and smiles that cocky, smug grin I don't get enough of, as if to say, "So what?"

**What He Did to her Daughter**

The best picture I have of Great-Aunt P
is her 250 pounds cinched into a turquoise dress
of fluttery silk at a cousin's wedding.
Her blond hair is controlled in an upsweep
over her voluptuous Bridgette Bardot pout
and she even looks demure because there's no sound
and her sailor-mouth is closed.

Sorry, but I don't actually know
what her son-in-law said or did—
that large hulk of a man
at least a foot taller than her.

Whatever it was
it built a whirlwind inside Aunt P,
threw her arm back in an arc
like a pitcher winding up
and lifted her
in a gravity-defying leap
that planted her fist into his cheek
in one solid graceful motion
her turquoise dress flouncing around her.

Yeah, I wish I remembered why too.

**For My Cousin Frances**

after a thousand kisses by the coffin
after naval emissaries hand over the glory
and walk off the icy hillside

after the women gather plastic forks into cups
like bouquets from another planet

while perfume of the real flowers
lingers in the house

silence will descend with a crash.

## The Luxurious Clock

There's a boy riding an elephant
whose belly rests on a dark green clock
that sits on top of four legs
formed by elephant trunks.

There's a cousin on the couch
hair teased around a pretty face
set with a permanent pout.

Another cousin in a chair
with the strand of air
wrapped around her face
while she presses her hands
against the flue of life
striving not to fall through.

There's a mother also on the couch
smiling through another story
about some comeuppance
she has delivered.

There's a writer at the table
who patters on her computer
to record the scene
that trembles and prepares to fade
once the mother dies.

At the chime,
she glances from the living room
to the boy on the elephant—
And now—poof! They're gone.

## Strikes of Lightening

In the once beautiful face
now swollen by disease and its cure,
her lips roll in and knead
and pull a twitch in my heart.

Her house will not stand a year.
Its Chinese statues and cut glass
will scatter, her children will flounder
in a tsunami of lost faith—
the hub of their world broken.

**Exquisite Taste**

Elena brought her friends to her parents' house
and bent over to kiss her cousin visiting from the country.
"Oh, it's been so long. How is the new little man?"
Her voice was enthusiastic, her eyes focused on the new mother's
  limp hair.
A quick curved hand fell under her own perfect curls,
drawing a line of distinction.

Cursory introductions were disposed of politely
before Elena led her guests to more intriguing things.
She catalogued antiques in a modulated tone
with impassioned gestures.
She reported the history of the refurbished rooms
complete with injurious "before" photos. Her guests applauded,
then for many minutes stood before curved oak cabinets
silently watching Tiffany vases bloom behind the polished glass.

Their rapt attention was broken only
when the country cousin shuffled behind them
and Elena sang out, "Oh, I must see him soon."

The cousin nodded knowingly at the back of Elena's head
then climbed the stairs with a bottle.
She carried her infant out to the balcony
that hung close to Long Island Sound
and walked with him in the warm night breeze
while Elena and her guests
strolled the broad cement patio beneath her.

She watched Elena twirl so the breeze
moved her skirt the most graceful way
and saw her smile and point toward the beams of light
that swept intermittently from the lighthouse.

The smile was possessive
and the hand reached toward the beams
as if to grasp the light and draw it onto herself.

## At Her Aunt's House

Ok, honey, when you get there
keep your mouth shut—
don't give them more reason
to think less of us—
which won't be a problem
for several hours
because they'll describe the details
of their lives as if you were writing
a book about them.

Don't tell them how much you paid
for anything because they will squint at the thing
and squeeze out a sour smile so that you know
everything you wear is too cheap
or old fashioned for their taste.

Be sure to compliment Donny
On the swords in his room.
He has to have something to do,
poor boy. Nothing else in his life is working.

If you run out of things to talk about
and if he hasn't already bored you to death
with it, ask your uncle about his business
because that's always good for an hour or two.

Watch your aunt in the kitchen.
Ask her about what's she's doing
so she can give you advice
to bring home to your poor family.

And for God's sake, girl,
tell them all how much
I love and miss them.

**Reflection on a Fiction Character's Lilt**

it's infuriating that I can't find that line in a story
about a character's lilt
that made me listen to the voices in my past—

all those chunky voices that end high—
the same spot as the lilt—
but move to that point
not like flowers flipping on a breeze—
more like women lifting heavy baskets
to climb a mountain—

baskets full of words
whether laughter or thunder
tilting them high so even disaster
found itself malleable.

my own voices echo now
those of my grandmother and her sisters—
those Italian immigrant daughters—
how I miss their might and push
their ability to grow gumption—
the comfort of their chunky chuffles.